S0-ARG-612

This journal belongs to

....

Date

....

She is clothed with strength and dignity;
she can laugh at the days to come.

Proverbs 31:25

$\mathcal{Y}$ou are a beautiful woman of God, precious to Him in every way. As you seek Him, He will increase your strength by letting you lean on His never-ending affection. Let His presence cast out any weakness and guide you through every circumstance and decision you face. Use this journal to record that journey, to express your thoughts, to pour out your prayers, and in turn hear God's whispers of love and support.

Be strong in the Lord, and may His unfailing love guide your heart into a fearless future.

Stop looking back, your future isn't there. Stop trying to guard and protect your present. Your future isn't there. Look AHEAD and press forward! Focus on your future!

Sandi Krakowski

*Forgetting what is behind and straining toward what is ahead, I press on toward
the goal to win the prize for which God has called me heavenward in Christ Jesus.*

Philippians 3:13–14

It is God who arms me with strength, and makes my way perfect.

Psalm 18:32 NKJV

We don't have to be perfect.... We are asked only to be real,
trusting in His perfection to cover our imperfection,
knowing that one day we will finally be all that
Christ saved us for and wants us to be.

Gigi Graham Tchividjian

Confidence is not based on wishful thinking,
but in knowing that God is in control.

Hannah Whitall Smith

God causes everything to work together for the good of those who love God and are called according to his purpose for them.

Romans 8:28 NLT

This is the day that the LORD has made;
let us rejoice and be glad in it.

Psalm 118:24 ESV

Resolve to make every day count. Be a woman of action.
Treat each day as precious.

Emilie Barnes

I don't really want more time; I just want enough time.
Time to breathe deep and time to see real and time to laugh long,
time to give You glory and rest deep and sing joy.

Ann Voskamp

*I trust in you, O L*ORD*; I say, "You are my God." My times are in your hand.*

Psalm 31:14–15 ESV

You make known to me the path of life; you will fill me with joy in your presence, with eternal pleasures at your right hand.

Psalm 16:11

*Good humor and laughter are far too wonderful
not to come straight from the heart of God.*

Beth Moore

I was made for more than being stuck in a vicious cycle of defeat. I am not made to be a victim of my poor choices. I was made to be a victorious child of God.

Lysa TerKeurst

With God we will gain the victory.

Psalm 60:12

*Take delight in the LORD, and he will give you
your heart's desires.*

Psalm 37:4 NLT

God shines brightly through the soul that is wholly devoted to Him.
Satisfied in Him. Trusting in Him. Delighting in Him.

Angela Thomas

Courage isn't a feeling that you wait for. Courage is doing when you don't have courage. Courage is doing it scared.

Jill Briscoe

Do not fear, for I am with you; do not be dismayed, for I am your God.
I will strengthen you and help you; I will uphold you with my righteous right hand.

Isaiah 41:10

Not by might, nor by power, but by my Spirit,
says the Lord *of hosts.*

Zechariah 4:6 ESV

> *Our hero status is not dependent on our human might or power
> or even our human spirit; it comes from the power of His spirit.*
>
> Lisa Bevere

Nothing on earth is more fun and more full than being distributed by an all-knowing, compassionate God who knows exactly where our ridiculously blessed lives would be best spent.

Jennie Allen

....

....

....

....

....

....

....

....

....

....

....

....

....

....

If you extend your soul to the hungry and satisfy the afflicted soul, then your light shall dawn in the darkness, and your darkness shall be as the noonday. The Lord will guide you continually, and satisfy your soul in drought, and strengthen your bones.

Isaiah 58:10-11 NKJV

Whatever you do, work at it with all your heart.

Colossians 3:23 NIV

When I stand before God at the end of my life,
I would hope that I would not have a single bit of talent left,
and could say, "I used everything you gave me."

Erma Bombeck

There's a beauty to wisdom and experience that cannot be faked. It's impossible to be mature without having lived.

Amy Grant

As you received Christ Jesus the Lord, so walk in him, rooted and built up in him and established in the faith...abounding in thanksgiving.

Colossians 2:6–7 ESV

God's love has been poured out into our hearts through the Holy Spirit, who has been given to us.

Romans 5:5

When we keep in mind the amazing grace poured out on us,
our hearts are stirred to share God's grace with others.
Radiant women, we are His messengers, His ambassadors, and the
proclaimers entrusted with the good news of salvation.

Marian Jordan

Christ never was in a hurry. There was no rushing forward, no anticipating, no fretting over what might be. Each day's duties were done as each day brought them, and the rest was left with God.

Mary Slessor

Cast your burden on the LORD, and He shall sustain you.

Psalm 55:22 NKJV

May the God of hope fill you with all joy and peace as you trust in him,
so that you may overflow with hope by the power of the Holy Spirit.

Romans 15:13

Courage is not about knowing the path.
It is about taking the first step.

Katie J. Davis

Our days are in God's hands. He is all-sufficient to meet our needs, and the Savior is with us every step of the way.

Elizabeth George

My times are in your hands; deliver me from the hands of my enemies.

Psalm 31:15

The LORD will work out his plans for my life—
for your faithful love, O LORD, endures forever.

Psalm 138:8 NLT

*God does not change, but He uses change—to change us.
He sends us on journeys that bring us to the end of ourselves.
We often feel out of control, yet if we embrace His leading,
we may find ourselves on the ride of our lives.*

Jen Hatmaker

Smile...it kills time between disasters.

Barbara Johnson

The cheerful heart has a continual feast.

Proverbs 15:15

*In your strength I can crush an army;
with my God I can scale any wall.*

Psalm 18:29 NLT

Do not be satisfied with little things,
because God wants great things!

Catherine of Siena

God has promised us even more than His own Son. He's promised us power through the Spirit—power that will help us do all that He asks of us.

Joni Eareckson Tada

*Those who wait upon God get fresh strength. They spread their wings and soar
like eagles, they run and don't get tired, they walk and don't lag behind.*

Isaiah 40:31 MSG

The Lᴏʀᴅ *is my strength and my shield; my heart trusted in Him,*
and I am helped; therefore my heart greatly rejoices,
and with my song I will praise Him.

Psalm 28:7 ɴᴋᴊᴠ

The greatest honor we can give Almighty God is to live gladly because of the knowledge of His love.

Julian of Norwich

Never be passive. Victories happen when you take charge of a game.
You can't win by playing not to lose.

Karen Kingsbury

He makes my feet like the feet of a deer; he causes me to stand on the heights.
He trains my hands for battle; my arms can bend a bow of bronze.

Psalm 18:33–34

For the LORD God is a sun and shield; the LORD gives grace and glory;
no good thing does He withhold from those who walk uprightly.

Psalm 84:11 NASB

Keep your face to the sun and you will never see the shadows.

Helen Keller

God never permitted a difficulty to come into our life without also
giving us the ability to handle it. God has provided us with every faculty.
He has given us the power that we need for living victoriously.

Kathryn Kuhlman

Because you are my help, I sing in the shadow of your wings.
I cling to you; your right hand upholds me.

Psalm 63:7–8

Let's not allow ourselves to get fatigued doing good. At the right time we will harvest a good crop if we don't give up, or quit. Right now, therefore, every time we get the chance, let us work for the benefit of all, starting with the people closest to us in the community of faith.

Galatians 6:9–10 MSG

> *From Christ's perspective, success isn't measured by how much we do, how much we earn, or how much we have, but by how well we love and what kind of person we're becoming in the midst of life's activities.*
>
> Leslie Vernick

What one has to do usually can be done.

Eleanor Roosevelt

I can do all things through Christ, because he gives me strength.

Philippians 4:13 NCV

I pray that out of his glorious riches he may strengthen you with power through his Spirit in your inner being, so that Christ may dwell in your hearts through faith. And I pray that you, being rooted and established in love, may have power...to grasp how wide and long and high and deep is the love of Christ.

Ephesians 3:16–18

*Sad is contagious. But the upside is—love is too.
It even multiplies. The more love I see,
the more I think that love is its own Super Power.*

Chrissy Kelly

Courage might not be about bravery or doing something worthy of valor.
Courage, sometimes, might just be being present.

Sarah Markley

Have I not commanded you? Be strong and courageous. Do not be afraid;
do not be discouraged, for the LORD your God will be with you wherever you go.

Joshua 1:9

I will sing of your strength, in the morning I will sing of your love; for you are my fortress, my refuge in times of trouble. You are my strength, I sing praise to you; you, God, are my fortress, my God on whom I can rely.

Psalm 59:16–17

The dedicated life is the life worth living.
You must give with your whole heart.

Annie Dillard

Strength, rest, guidance, grace, help, sympathy,
love—all from God to us! What a list of blessings!

Evelyn Stenbock

I will sing to the LORD, because he has dealt bountifully with me.

Psalm 13:6 ESV

He said to me, "My grace is sufficient for you, for my power is made perfect in weakness." Therefore I will boast all the more gladly about my weaknesses, so that Christ's power may rest on me.

2 Corinthians 12:9

*In difficulties, I can drink freely of God's power
and experience His touch of refreshment and blessing—
much like an invigorating early spring rain.*

Anabel Gillham

As the chaos swirls and life's demands pull at me on all sides, I will breathe in God's peace that surpasses all understanding. He has promised that He would set within me a peace too deeply planted to be affected by unexpected or exhausting demands.

Wendy Moore

This is what the LORD says...“When you pass through the waters, I will be with you; and when you pass through the rivers, they will not sweep over you. When you walk through the fire, you will not be burned; the flames will not set you ablaze.”

Isaiah 43:1-2

O LORD, you hear the desire of the afflicted;
you will strengthen their heart.

Psalm 10:17 ESV

The word comfort is from two Latin words meaning
"with" and "strong"—He is with us to make us strong.
Comfort is not soft, weakening commiseration;
it is true, strengthening love.

Amy Carmichael

Each of us knows that we have an obligation to care for the old, the young, and the sick. We stand strongest when we stand with the weakest among us.

Sarah Palin

Two are better than one, because they have a good return for their work:
If one falls down, his friend can help him up.

Ecclesiastes 4:9-10

Your right hand has held me up, Your gentleness has made me great.

Psalm 18:35 NKJV

When a woman feels truly loved, she is confident in herself,
she is more generous of heart to be able to reach others,
and her faith grows strong because of the deep acceptance
she receives and lives in from her Creator.

Sally Clarkson

God longs to give favor—that is, spiritual strength and health—to those who seek Him, and Him alone. He grants spiritual favors and victories, not because the one who seeks Him is holier than anyone else, but in order to make His holy beauty and His great redeeming power known.

Teresa of Avila

Look to the L<small>ORD</small> *and his strength; seek his face always.*

1 Chronicles 16:11

Do not be afraid. Stand firm and you will see the deliverance the LORD will bring you today.... The LORD will fight for you; you need only to be still.

Exodus 14:13-14

There is the firm commitment to the triumph of the human spirit over adversity, the certainty that there's a God on high who may not move mountains but will give you the strength to climb.

Geneva Smitherman

We are to do what He is unfolding for us to do, fulfilling what God is giving us strength to do, acknowledging that it is His strength and not ours.

Edith Schaeffer

The Lord is my strength and my defense; he has become my salvation.
He is my God, and I will praise him.

Exodus 15:2

I pray that from his glorious, unlimited resources he will empower you with inner strength through his Spirit. Then Christ will make his home in your hearts as you trust in him. Your roots will grow down into God's love and keep you strong.

Ephesians 3:16–17 NLT

The truth is, we try to face life's struggles and temptations in our own strength, and it just doesn't work. There are some things we just cannot battle on our own. We must connect to our life source, the Vine, our Lord, on a daily basis, for much-needed spiritual nourishment.

Debby Mayne

God has given me His strength, for which I am grateful. His joy fills my days, so I have no trouble laughing at the days to come, for which I'm also grateful.

Diann Hunt

He will yet fill your mouth with laughter and your lips with shouts of joy.

Job 8:21

*Be glad in the LORD, and rejoice, O righteous, and shout for joy,
all you upright in heart!*

Psalm 32:11 ESV

Gratitude helps you to grow and expand; gratitude brings joy and laughter into your life and into the lives of all those around you.

Eileen Caddy

If the Lord calls us to be a bridge, we have to learn to bear in His strength the weight. And it hurts. And it's good. And the Lord equips.

Rosaria Champagne Butterfield

The Spirit God gave us does not make us timid,
but gives us power, love and self-discipline.

2 Timothy 1:7

You, O Lord, are a shield about me,
my glory, and the lifter of my head.

Psalm 3:3 ESV

Difficulty is inevitable. Drama is a choice.

Anita Renfroe

Hope has an astonishing resilience and strength. Its very persistence in our hearts indicates that it is not a tonic for wishful thinkers but the ground on which realists stand.

Kathleen Norris

I...ask the God of our Master, Jesus Christ...to make you intelligent and discerning in knowing him personally, your eyes focused and clear, so that you can...grasp the immensity of this glorious way of life he has for his followers, oh, the utter extravagance of his work in us who trust him—endless energy, boundless strength!

Ephesians 1:18–19 MSG

The wise prevail through great power,
and those who have knowledge muster their strength.

Proverbs 24:5

*Doing the right thing causes us to stand taller, dance more often,
and step into life with more confidence.*

Patsy Clairmont

You are more than a conqueror, you are beautiful inside and out, and the Lord God Almighty has a very bright future in store for you because you are His princess now and forever!

CeCe Winans

....

....

....

....

....

....

....

....

....

....

....

....

....

....

In all these things we are more than conquerors through him who loved us.

Romans 8:37

*Whether you eat or drink, or whatever you do,
do all to the glory of God.*

1 Corinthians 10:31 NKJV

I have one desire now—to live a life of reckless abandon for the Lord, putting all my energy and strength into it.

Elisabeth Elliot

A quiet morning with a loving God puts the events of the upcoming day into proper perspective.

Janette Oke

Let us look only to Jesus, the One who began our faith and who makes it perfect. He suffered death on the cross. But he accepted the shame as if it were nothing because of the joy that God put before him. And now he is sitting at the right side of God's throne.

Hebrews 12:2 NCV

Those who are wise will shine like the brightness of the heavens.

Daniel 12:3

Reject low living, sight walking, small planning, casual praying, and limited giving—God has chosen you for greatness.

Anne Graham Lotz

Every evening I turn my worries over to God.
He's going to be up all night anyway.

Mary C. Crowley

Give all your worries to him, because he cares about you.

1 Peter 5:7 NCV

The steadfast love of the Lord *never ceases;*
his mercies never come to an end; they are new every morning;
great is your faithfulness.

Lamentations 3:22–23 ESV

You and I can go to God when we are too tired, too lazy, too uncommitted, too sick, or feeling too sorry for ourselves. In fact, moments like these are precisely when we need to call upon God and be filled with His faithfulness.

Elizabeth George

A Christian has no business being satisfied with mediocrity.
She's supposed to reach for the stars. Why not?
She's not on her own anymore. She has God's help now.

Catherine Marshall

*Surely God is my salvation; I will trust and not be afraid. The L*ORD*, the L*ORD *himself, is my strength and my defense; he has become my salvation.*

Isaiah 12:2

*Blessed be the Lord, who daily bears our burden,
the God who is our salvation.*

Psalm 68:19 NASB

Fight the urge to spread yourself too thin.
Hone in on what matters today.

Priscilla Shirer

Freedom is what we were made for! We are designed to live out our destiny in partnership with God—to live every day and every year with bigger dreams. We really can change the world!

Beni Johnson and Sheri Silk

*Let your light shine before others, that they may see
your good deeds and glorify your Father in heaven.*

Matthew 5:16

How blessed all those in whom you live, whose lives become roads you travel;
they wind through lonesome valleys, come upon brooks, discover cool
springs and pools brimming with rain! God-traveled, these roads
curve up the mountain, and at the last turn—Zion! God in full view!

Psalm 84:5-7 MSG

The most beautiful women I've ever observed are those that have exchanged a self-focused life for a Christ-focused one. They are confident, but not in themselves. Instead of self-confidence, they radiate with Christ-confidence.

Leslie Ludy

Every experience God gives us, every person He puts in our lives is the perfect preparation for the future that only He can see.

Corrie ten Boom

*His divine power has given us everything we need for a godly life through
our knowledge of him who called us by his own glory and goodness.*

1 Peter 1:3

You turned my wailing into dancing; you removed my sackcloth and clothed me with joy, that my heart may sing your praises and not be silent. Lord my God, I will praise you forever.

Psalm 30:11-12

Laughter lightens your load and lifts your heart into heavenly places. Your laughter rises to heaven and blends with angelic melodies of praise.

Sarah Young

We must drink deeply from the very Source the deep calm and peace of interior quietude and refreshment of God, allowing the pure water of divine grace to flow plentifully and unceasingly from the Source itself.

Mother Teresa

Blessed is the one who trusts in the Lord, whose confidence is in him.
They will be like a tree planted by the water that sends out its roots by the stream.
It does not fear when heat comes; its leaves are always green.
It has no worries in a year of drought and never fails to bear fruit.

Jeremiah 17:7–8

*She opens her mouth in wisdom, and the teaching
of kindness is on her tongue.*

Proverbs 31:26 NASB

Little deeds of kindness, little words of love,
help to make earth happy like the heaven above.

Julia Fletcher Carney

Character cannot be developed in ease and quiet. Only through experience of trial and suffering can the soul be strengthened, ambition inspired, and success achieved.
Helen Keller

After you have suffered a little while, [God] will himself restore you
and make you strong, firm and steadfast.

1 Peter 5:10

As iron sharpens iron, so one person sharpens another.

Proverbs 27:17

Not only do we need others for the joy of friendship, love, and fun, but we need each other to stay sharp.

Trish Perry

You must learn day by day, year by year to broaden your horizon.
The more things you love, the more you are interested in,
the more you enjoy, the more you are indignant about,
the more you have left when anything happens.

Ethel Barrymore

*People should eat and drink and enjoy the fruits of their labor,
for these are gifts from God.*

Ecclesiastes 3:13 NLT

May the righteous be glad and rejoice before God;
may they be happy and joyful.

Psalm 68:3

Life is too short to be anything but real with the cast of characters God has placed in the story of your life. Love well, laugh often, and find your life in Christ.

Karen Kingsbury

The Lord's chief desire is to reveal Himself to you and, in order for Him to do that, He gives you abundant grace. The Lord gives you the experience of enjoying His presence. He touches you, and His touch is so delightful that, more than ever, you are drawn inwardly to Him.

Madame Jeanne Guyon

Out of his fullness we have all received grace in place of grace already given.

John 1:16

*The Lord will be your confidence and will
keep your foot from being caught.*

Proverbs 3:26 ESV

Confidence is not based on wishful thinking,
but in knowing that God is in control. There are no
hidden reserves in the promises of God that are meant
to deprive them of their complete fulfillment.

Hannah Whitall Smith

We know that [God] gives us every grace, every abundant grace; and though we are so weak of ourselves, this grace is able to carry us through every obstacle and difficulty.

Elizabeth Ann Seton

Let us then approach God's throne of grace with confidence, so that we may receive mercy and find grace to help us in our time of need.

Hebrews 4:16

Satisfy us in the morning with your unfailing love,
that we may sing for joy and be glad all our days.

Psalm 90:14

Every day we live is a priceless gift of God, loaded with possibilities to learn something new, to gain fresh insights.

Dale Evans Rogers

Spending time with God is the key to our strength and success in all areas of life. Be sure that you never try to work God into your schedule, but always work your schedule around Him.

Joyce Meyer

I have set the L<small>ORD</small> *always before me;*
because he is at my right hand I shall not be shaken.

Psalm 16:8 <small>ESV</small>

O God, you are my God; earnestly I seek you;
my soul thirsts for you; my flesh faints for you,
as in a dry and weary land where there is no water.

Psalm 63:1 ESV

Are you weak? Weary? Confused? Troubled? Pressured?
How is your relationship with God? Is it held in its place
of priority? I believe the greater the pressure,
the greater your need for time alone with Him.

Kay Arthur

*Life isn't about how to survive the storm;
it's about how to dance in the rain.*

Even though the fig trees have no blossoms, and there are no grapes on the vines;
even though the olive crop fails, and the fields lie empty and barren...yet I will rejoice
in the Lᴏʀᴅ! I will be joyful in the God of my salvation!

Habakkuk 3:17–18 ɴʟᴛ

God's blessings make life rich; nothing we do can improve on God.

Proverbs 10:22 MSG

*Friendship, love, health, energy, enthusiasm, and joy
are the things that make life worth living and exploring.*

Denise Austin

Faith is what makes life bearable, with all its tragedies and ambiguities and sudden, startling joys.

Madeleine L'Engle

*Though you have not seen him, you love him; and even though you do not see him now,
you believe in him and are filled with an inexpressible and glorious joy, for you
are receiving the end result of your faith, the salvation of your souls.*

1 Peter 1:8–9

Trust in the LORD and do good;
dwell in the land and enjoy safe pasture.

Psalm 37:3

We have, by God's grace, been given another day to serve and love, laugh and learn, pray and ponder. Spring is ready to burst into the open air, and we are ready to embrace it.

Rosaria Champagne Butterfield

Joy planted by the Holy Spirit is eternal, forever, and never-ending.
True joy happens in the heart of a Christian because it springs from
knowing that God loves me and wants what is best for me.

Dannah Gresh

Don't be dejected and sad, for the joy of the LORD is your strength!

Nehemiah 8:10 NLT

Whatever you do, whether in word or deed, do it all in the name of the Lord Jesus, giving thanks to God the Father through him.

Colossians 3:17

A woman with a confident heart chooses to believe that God wants to make an impact through her life, and she looks for ways to let Him.

Renee Swope

*When you know who you really are, you glow with an inner radiance
and confidence that affects every other part of your life.*

Nancy Stafford

Those who look to him are radiant; their faces are never covered with shame.

Psalm 34:5

Be strong in the Lord and in his mighty power.

Ephesians 6:10

WOMEN OF JOY™

The world moves so fast, sometimes you need a little time to break away. Our friends at Women of Joy have been encouraging women with the Word of God, the joy of music, and the spirit of friendship through Women of Joy Weekends for more than a decade. Offering teaching and worship, with time for fun sprinkled in, you will be amazed at what a difference forty-eight hours with a group of women, friends, or daughters can make.
Visit www.womenofjoy.org for more information.

...inspired by life
EllieClaire.com

At Ellie Claire® Gift & Paper Expressions, we are passionate about living life beyond the ordinary. We invite you to use our products to express your thoughts, record your prayers, embrace your dreams, and find encouragement in a life inspired by joy. Discover more Ellie Claire journals, devotionals, and gift books at EllieClaire.com.

Ellie Claire® Gift & Paper Expressions
Franklin, TN 37067
EllieClaire.com
Ellie Claire is registered trademark of Worthy Media, Inc.

She Is Clothed with Strength and Dignity Journal
© 2014 by Ellie Claire
Published by Ellie Claire, an imprint of Worthy Publishing Group, a division of Worthy Media, Inc. in partnership with
Women of Joy

Women of Joy has been encouraging women with the Word of God, the joy of music, and the spirit of friendship for
more than a decade. They offer conferences nationwide to help women connect with each other and experience God in
a new and stronger way. Visit www.womenofjoy.org for more information.

ISBN 978-1-63326-008-5

Stock or custom editions of Ellie Claire titles may be purchased in bulk for
educational, business, ministry, fundraising, or sales promotional use. For
information, please e-mail info@EllieClaire.com

Compiled by Jill Jones
Cover and interior design by Gearbox | studiogearbox.com

Printed in China

4 5 6 7 8 9 10 11 12 – 20 19 18 17 16 15